How to Care for Your Hamster

CONTENTS

Photographs by:
Colin Jeal, Frank Naylor

©2001 by Kingdom Books PO9 5TL ENGLAND

PREFACE

The hamster most often offered for sale in pet shops is the Golden Hamster, known to science as *Mesocricetus auratus*. Just one litter was discovered in Syria around 1930 but the hamster now is one of the most popular small pets in Great Britain.

Dwarf hamsters, genus *Phodopus*, are also gaining in popularity among hobbyists. These attractive little animals are about a third of the size of the Golden Hamster. Their requirements are a little different from those of the Syrian or Golden Hamster which is the animal that we are discussing in this book.

Appearance

The hamster resembles a tiny bear: it is easy to see this when it rears up on its hind legs and dances around. Usually the hair is dense and sleek unless, of course, it is a Long-haired or Rex variety. There is not much hair on the stomach compared to the fur on the upper side of the body. The head, once narrow and rat-like, has grown broader and shorter with selective breeding. There are four toes and a primitive thumb on each front leg. These look rather like baby human hands but, in fact, the feet are well adapted for digging and climbing and have sharp claws. The five digits on the back feet are fully developed. The strong muscles of the hind legs enabled the hamster to crawl backwards as well as forwards through the narrow passages which made up its burrow in the wild. Its short legs make the hamster walk with a decided waddle. The eyes are shiny and bold; the ears are large and erect. The tail is almost, but not quite, missing, being about 2.5cm long, and it is sparsely covered with short hair.

The hamster's most fascinating feature is its cheek pouches, into which it can stuff a truly incredible amount of food. When the pouches are full, the hamster's head balloons to double its size and it resembles no other animal in the world. These pouches are located on the sides of the head, neck and shoulders and have no connection with the digestive organs. When relaxed, the pouches are about 2.5cm deep but when crammed with food they extend to at least 5cm. This unbelievable stretching power has caused many owners, on first seeing their new pet's full pouches, to call the vet to announce that their hamster has mumps! When it wants to empty the pouches, the hamster simply leans forward and pushes them with its tiny hands, depositing the hoarded treasure in some favourite hiding place. Just as the hamster's pouches stretch, so does its skin, which fits loosely over the whole body.

The hamster, being a rodent, is well equipped with gnawing teeth. It also has strong jaws to help it gnaw. The teeth are unusual: they extend far into the jaw and grow out at a rate that compensates for the wear resulting from the hamster's constant eating and gnawing. In fact, since a hamster's teeth never stop growing, it is important that it is given appropriate chew items to gnaw on, such as dog biscuits, to prevent its teeth from overgrowing. There are four rodent-like incisor teeth to cut with, as well as molars to grind the food. Only the fronts of the teeth are enamelled which means that the backs wear down more quickly. The remaining enamel forms a sharp cutting edge which the hamster uses to gnaw roots, wood and other tough material.

It is not difficult to differentiate between males and females. Looking down on them from above, the male's body is elongated, presenting a tapered rear view, while the rear of the female is blunter. Also, the female is usually larger and heavier than the male, averaging about 2.5cm to 5cm longer and 55g to 85g heavier.

Colour Variation

More and more colour variations are being seen as a result of mutations and selective breeding. Some of those more commonly seen are the Cream, the Cinnamon, the Albino, the Sable, the Dominant Spotted, the Grey and the Yellow, but many more colours are available. Hamsters differ only in colour, not in size or conformation. Considering the comprehensive efforts of today's hamster breeders, no doubt the future selective breeding of hamsters will yield an even greater assortment of colour varieties.

There are also different coat varieties in the Golden Hamster. These include Short-hair, Long-hair, Satin (a particularly glossy coat, which can be seen on any coat variety and colour) and the wavy-haired Rex (Short-hair, Long-hair or Satin).

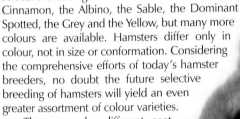

An alert Golden Banded Hamster.

SELECTION

When you are buying a hamster (or any other pet) it is always wise to go to a reputable pet shop or breeder. Good hamsters are not that expensive so you do not have to look for bargains. Nor should you buy from a private person unless you know what you are getting. An untamed or badly tamed hamster will only disappoint you, and there is always the possibility that an unknown hamster may be ill-tempered because of bad treatment. The wisest procedure is to select a healthy young animal and train it yourself.

Look for one between five and eight weeks old. Baby hamsters are very shy and easily frightened so it is useless to try to tame one until it is a little, but not too much, older. Also you should remember that the hamster's natural lifespan is only about two years, although the odd animal can reach the age of three, and so you will be able to enjoy yours for a longer time if you get it soon after it has been weaned.

Take your time as you make your decision. Ask the breeder or pet shop assistant to show you as many animals as you want to examine. You will want to make sure that your choice is in good physical condition with an easy-going disposition. Care now may very well prevent problems later on.

First look for signs of good health: soft clean fur, bright clear eyes, and a general feel of solidity. Avoid bony or skinny animals. Look at the ears which will give you a good idea of the hamster's age. In a young hamster, the insides of the ears are covered with tiny white hairs. These gradually disappear with age and, when the animal is older, the ears are hairless and shiny. Some hamsters may have nicks in their ears. This is usually a sign that they have been in a fight but, if the nicks are clean and healed, it is nothing to worry about.

After examining the ears, look at the nose, feet and belly. There should be no sores or crusty scabs, which indicate either skin problems or fighting. Avoid any animal with a runny nose or watery eyes, or one that is lethargic and dull. A wet tail is also a sign of poor health. Make sure there are no scars or bald patches in the fur. Do not worry, however, if you see small spots about a centimetre in diameter on the hips. They may be either flesh coloured or black, and feel much thicker than the rest of the skin. They are called dimorphic pigment spots and are perfectly normal.

One Or Two?

How many animals you want depends, of course, on your requirements. Do you want to breed hamsters or do you want one just as a pet? Since they are solitary creatures by nature, you do not have to worry that one hamster will be lonely by itself. As long as it gets a reasonable amount of affection from you, it will be perfectly happy to live alone. If you do want more than one hamster, they cannot be housed together in the same cage after they are six weeks old, except when you want to breed them.

A Long-haired Sable Banded Hamster investigates its surroundings.

Male Or Female?

The sex is not that important if you decide to have only one animal. The females have a tendency to grow less friendly as they get older, whereas males are more likely to remain docile. A pregnant female may be a bit more snappy; however, this is true of the females of most species. If you do pick a female, check her carefully to make sure that she is not pregnant. Ask the dealer to confirm this for you. If she is nearly ready to give birth her condition will be fairly obvious.

A less prominent bulge in her stomach can be detected by comparing her with other females nearby, unless she was mated so recently that she has not yet started to gain weight. The best way to ensure that you do not buy a pregnant female is to pick a female no older than five or six weeks that has been kept away from the males.

Choosing

Do not choose a hamster just by observing it in the cage. Ask the breeder or pet shop assistant to put it on a counter or table where you can take a closer look. Do not try to take it out of the cage yourself. Look carefully how the seller does it.

When the hamster has been placed on the table, do not try to pick it up. Give it a chance to become acquainted with you, perhaps by offering it a titbit. As hamsters are very inquisitive, this should bring it to you in no time. Once it seems to be used to you, extend your hand slowly and offer the titbit. Remember that it is still nervous; do not make any sudden moves. If the hamster does not scurry away, slowly move your outstretched hand over and around it, then grip gently but firmly around the entire body so that the hamster is cradled in your closed fist. Never reach down from above and pick up a hamster suddenly: you are sure to be nipped. Some owners prefer to pick up their pets by bringing their hands together, palms up, on either side of their animals and then scooping them up into their open hands. When you have managed to pick it up, inspect it for the points I have discussed above. If the hamster is difficult to pick up, afraid or tries to bite, select another animal and follow the same procedure.

Do not be too hasty when choosing your hamster friend, but do not ignore your heart totally. You want your new pet to be both healthy and happy.

A bright-eyed, alert hamster explores a lump of tree bark. Make sure there are no poisonous chemicals contaminating wood or tree bark given to hamsters.

The hamster does not require a great deal of maintenance, but the few things it does need are essential, and you have to make sure that they are provided.

Pet shops stock many types of cages designed especially for hamsters. The most convenient of the mass-produced cages are those with plastic bases and wire canopies. These are easy to keep clean and come in various sizes. Buy the largest cage that you can afford. The hamster is an active little creature who likes to move around. It will become nervous and snappy if confined for long in a cage which is too small for it, because it will not get enough exercise.

I would recommend a cage at least 60cm x 45cm x 30cm. It is better not to buy a cage with more than two levels, as a hamster can injure itself badly by falling between different levels. Another good home is a glass aquarium tank, with minor adaptations. You will have to fit a wire-mesh lid to the top.

The cage should be deeply padded with a good absorbent material such as wood shavings or a commercially-prepared hamster litter. Avoid any bedding material which might irritate or scratch cheek pouches. Never use old woollen blankets or other fabrics to line a hamster's cage as the animal will chew and swallow them, upsetting its digestion. Moreover, the fabric will quickly become wet and dirty and will not be as easy to dispose of as wood shavings. Do not use newspaper because the print is toxic.

Next you need a feeding dish and a hamster water bottle that hangs from the side of the cage. The feeding dish does not have to be very large but it should be fastened securely to the side of the cage so that it cannot be knocked over. Alternatively, you can use a heavy earthenware bowl. The water bottle is necessary because the hamster will soon have a soggy cage if it is given water in an open dish. A suitable water bottle can be bought at pet shops.

To make sure that your pet gets plenty of exercise, buy a cage equipped with an exercise wheel or buy a wheel separately and install it yourself. For a Golden Hamster, the wheel should measure no less than 13cm in diameter. Another thing which your hamster will enjoy tremendously is a slide; you will enjoy watching it very much as well. Hamsters love to play with these toys and the exercise is good for them.

Your hamster should always have a branch of hardwood or fruit wood to nibble at. This not only helps to keep its teeth clean but also keeps them worn down to their proper length. If you have reason to believe that your pet's claws have grown too long, clip them with manicure scissors or nail clippers. Be careful not to cut into the quick, the blood vessel that runs down the centre of each claw.

When choosing a place in which to set up the cage, find somewhere that is warm and free from draughts. The cage should be in a room with a relatively constant temperature otherwise the hamster is likely to catch cold. Remember also that the hamster is a nocturnal animal. Given the choice it will sleep during the day and begin its activities after the sun has gone down. If the temperature drops too much at night it will not feel like moving around and may even

A group of Russian Piebald Hamsters. Piebald continues to be a popular variety.

A typical hamster cage set-up. From the left: nest box, exercise wheel, food bowl and water bottle.

Hamsters are naturally curious, always trying to escape and investigate further afield.

hibernate. Since the hamster is nocturnal its cage should be kept in a dark corner so that it can rest during the day. Do not keep the cage in the sun. The hamster's eyes are not designed for exposure to strong light and, if you keep the cage in a bright spot, you will seldom see your pet because it will stay hidden in its nest or buried in the shavings.

Care Of The Cage

You should clean out the hamster's cage thoroughly at least once a week. During the cleaning you will find stored-away food. Remove some, especially if it is rotting, but not all because this will upset your pet and it will rush around the cage for some time looking for it. Put the food back where you found it. This is true as well of the little wads of bedding that you will find. Put them back after each cleaning. The hamster does not like having to make its bed any more than most people do and it will be greatly annoyed if it has to begin all over again.

The hamster is a very clean animal and does not like to soil its living area. It will leave its droppings, which are hard and dry, in one area and urinate in a corner of the cage as far from the nest as possible. You should clean out this corner each day and put in new litter. Some owners make their lives even easier by using a large jar with a mouth wide enough for the hamster to enter. They lay this jar on its side in the corner of the cage which the hamster prefers for urination. The hamster uses the jar as its toilet and the floor of the cage stays dry. The jar should be washed out daily.

Make sure that the hamster's feeding dish is kept scrupulously clean. You must also wash out the water bottle every day by flushing it with fresh water and using a bottle brush if you see any build-up of algae.

FEEDING

The hamster is no great problem to feed as it will eat just about anything. Commercially-prepared hamster food is available from most pet shops and supplies the vitamins and minerals that your pet needs to stay healthy. This usually consists of a mix of pellets, sunflower seeds, peanuts and mixed flakes, and it should be used as the staple element of your pet's daily ration. In an

Your hamster will enjoy the occasional treat but nuts are very fattening and should not be given in excess.

A hamster uses its front paws to hold its food while it is eating.

emergency, you can temporarily substitute poultry grain, dry dog or cat food, bird seed, dry bread or breakfast cereal but you should return to the prepared food as soon as possible. A half kilo bag of this food will keep the average hamster supplied for about a month.

Do not give your pet too much fresh fruit or vegetables. While it needs some of the vitamins they contain, you should not give them more than once or twice a week. Make sure that any fruit and vegetables that you offer to your pet are fresh; always wash them thoroughly before you put them in the cage. They may have been sprayed with insecticides which are harmful to hamsters. Do not give your pet more fresh food than it can eat in a day. Spoiled foods can result in intestinal disturbances. As far as possible, avoid any foods which contain a high percentage of water. This is true of milk as well. While milk contributes to a hamster's growth, sometimes it has an unpredictable effect on the digestion.

A Golden Banded Hamster.

Your hamster will appreciate table scraps such as potato, pasta, egg, rice and even meat and fish, as long as the food is not spicy. The main reason for giving dry food is that hamsters do hoard, and moist foods decay and generate harmful bacteria.

The important thing to remember is that, like yourself, your hamster wants variety in its diet. Even though the commercial foods are excellent, pamper your pet at times by giving it a small treat of sunflower seeds or fresh fruit. It will make taming and training easier if you use these treats as rewards.

It is very entertaining to watch a hamster at feeding time. It will scurry over to the feeding dish to inspect the bill of fare, then begin to stuff the food into its cheek pouches. When its head has expanded to about twice its usual size, the hamster will disappear to unload its treasure wherever it has hidden its hoard. As soon as it has disposed of the first lot it will return for another.

After it has finished, it will come out of the nest and stand at the door brushing its nose with its little hands and grooming itself like a cat. A hamster prefers to eat without an audience and will do so later at its own convenience. All it cares about at first is gathering up as much food as it can and storing it away.

It is amusing to watch the hamster stuffing its cheek pouches and so there is a temptation to feed it often. There is no harm in this. By nature, a hamster is a frugal animal and will not over-eat, no matter how much food you supply. Neither will it eat all the food at once, preferring to hide what you give and nibble on it throughout the day. The best time to feed a hamster is in the early evening; this is the time when it is most active. Establish a regular feeding routine and stick to it. In this way the hamster learns that it will be fed at a certain time and comes to expect it. One feed a day is enough.

In the desert, the native hamster obtains most of its water from leafy plants. It does not need very much but you should fill its water bottle with fresh water every day. Another tip is always to return the food bowl to the same place. Hamsters are creatures of habit and anything out of order displeases them.

Some hamsters like live food as well. They have been known to eat ants, woodlice, cockroaches, flies and even wasps.

There are a few things you should not give a hamster for food, such as any of the acid fruits like oranges or grapefruit. Nor should you give it needles of evergreens, either as food or bedding. Hamsters do not like garlic and onions make them cross!

One of the advantages of owning a hamster is that it can take care of itself if you are going to be away from home. Make sure the water bottle is freshly filled, or even use two, and put a large supply of dry food in the cage. Your pet will be able to manage alone for a couple of days but it is against the law for it to be left completely for more than two days.

TAMING

A new hamster is a nervous animal. When first you bring it home, make sure that it is not frightened by someone moving suddenly or talking loudly. Leave your new pet completely alone for the first few days unless it shows that it wants to be friendly.

When you get it home, open the transport carrier very carefully. You will probably find the hamster has burrowed down in the litter. Do not thrust your hand in suddenly as it is likely to get nipped. First let the hamster see the back of your hand. Then slip your hand gently but firmly around the shoulders, so that the hamster's head lies in the palm facing your wrist. Quickly place it in its cage which, of course, you have prepared in advance. Make sure that the water bottle and feed dish are full, and then leave your pet alone, observing it from a distance. Remember that a hamster has a sensitive nervous system and that strange sounds and voices will frighten it.

A Russian Hamster.

Only when the hamster has accepted its surroundings and set up housekeeping, so to speak, should you attempt to become acquainted. It will make its bed, find a spot for its pantry, and choose a corner as the 'bathroom'. The female is usually more fussy about this than the male who is inclined to be lazy.

Taming is a simple procedure. It is only a matter of gaining your hamster's confidence. By nature it is a gentle, friendly animal and you, too, must be gentle and friendly, as well as patient. Patience is particularly important. If you try to hurry things, you will only frighten your pet and have to begin all over again.

A Cinnamon Hamster in 'teddy-bear' pose.

A Russian Hamster.

A Black Banded Hamster.

First, slowly put your hand into the cage. Offer your pet a titbit such as a sunflower seed, a peanut or a raisin, in the palm of your hand. Although the hamster may seem shy at first, its natural curiosity will overcome its nervousness, and it will come over to investigate and then start nibbling. Now try stroking it very gently.

When you feel that the hamster is calm enough to be picked up, do it in the manner described above; lift it out of the cage and place it on a table. However, you have to watch it closely. Hamsters have poor vision and yours might walk right over the edge. Like most other ground-dwelling animals, they have no instinctive fear of falling. A hamster is not able to turn its body in mid-air like a cat, so a fall can hurt it badly.

Stroke it gently and talk softly to it, using its name. A hamster will learn the sound of its name in quite a short time. Do this as often as possible until your pet gets completely used to you. Then you can place your hand on the table and let the hamster climb onto you.

Next, unless you have a dog or cat, put your hamster on the floor and let it wander around. Keep a close eye on it, however. Remember that it is a small creature that can crawl into tiny spaces and you may have trouble finding it again. Remember, too, that hamsters like to gnaw, so keep your eye on the furniture, electric cables and telephone wires.

Generally speaking, a hamster is rather timid, but sometimes it will become unruly, possibly to impress on you its courage and freedom from inhibition. If you are nervous about handling your hamster and always use gloves to do so, you will find that your pet becomes vicious. Fear causes a person to perspire, and apparently hamsters can detect fear through their sense of smell. The scent of this perspiration causes the hamster to become irritable and, when aroused, it will scamper about, turn on its back, bare its teeth, voice its war cry and generally act aggressively. An animal behaving like this can be gentled within two or three days if an unafraid person gives it special attention, quieting its fears and suspicions. A person who is unafraid, who likes animals and treats them with gentle firmness, will have no trouble at all.

Bad behaviour also can be a result of physical discomfort, unclean or uncomfortable bedding or illness. It can also be caused by noise or excitement, too much handling or being handled by a stranger. Biting is a natural reflex when any animal is frightened or startled.

TRAINING

Once your hamster has become completely tame, you can start teaching it to do tricks. Having a pet that can perform is a never-ending source of pride and amusement. Patience, perseverance and repetition are the keys to success in the training of any animal, hamsters included. How well you are able to train yours depends on how well you apply these three rules and on how much imagination you bring to the training process.

It is extremely important to use a reward. This reward should be a treat that your particular hamster really enjoys, perhaps a peanut, raisin or piece of fruit. Hold the treat above the hamster's head high enough so that it has to stand on its hind legs to reach it. Repeat its name and the command 'stand' until it does, and then give the reward. Repeat this procedure and the command again and again until the hamster stands whenever you hold your hand over its head, even without the reward. It will soon come to associate the word 'stand' with the act of standing up and do so whenever asked.

Teach your hamster its name using the same method. Hold out a morsel of food and call its name. It will come for the food and, after a number of repetitions, will begin to understand that the name refers to it. You can teach other commands in the same way but always remember to repeat the identical word and procedure.

There are no short cuts to training. As I said before, patience, perseverance and repetition are the keys. If you fail at first, don't be discouraged. Don't say, 'My hamster's too stupid' but keep on trying until you succeed. Your hamster, like any animal, can learn only through constant repetition. If you try to hurry the process, you will make it nervous and the training will be that much more difficult. Be gentle, keep your voice low and don't give up.

A Hamster Playground

Hamsters love to play and if you provide a playground you will find that you spend many happy hours watching their amusing antics. There are a great many toys on the market designed especially for hamsters. I have mentioned exercise wheels and slides but use your imagination and give your hamster things to climb on or wriggle through. Make a maze out of cardboard tubes with a reward at the end and see how long it takes before the hamster figures out the route.

Give your hamster lots of different things to do. It will enjoy playing and will be kept interested and active.

BREEDING

Until hamsters were first domesticated in the 1930s it was assumed that, at 23 days, rats and mice had the shortest gestation period of any animal. The female hamster, however, easily breaks that record with her gestation period of 16 days. She can have her first litter when she is only eight weeks old and then, if birth control is non-existent, have a litter almost every month for the rest of the year, with an average of seven babies each time. In that same year her children, grandchildren and great-grandchildren may also start to have litters.

This is what you must keep in mind if you decide to breed hamsters. Count the cages you will have to buy, the nest and cage litter, and the food. What will you do with all the babies? Breeding hamsters is not an enterprise to be entered into lightly. Unless you're ready, willing and able to take on a large task, keep your males and females apart.

Although the average female is capable of breeding at eight weeks it is wiser to wait until she is about three months old for her first mating. She will then be better able to withstand the strain of pregnancy and nursing her young.

In the wild, hamsters have a definite mating season but there is no season in the unnatural environment in which they are kept as pets. While they breed throughout the year, most litters are produced between May and November; in their wild state they are inactive and in semi-hibernation during the winter and early spring. The female's oestrus cycle (period of sexual heat) repeats itself every four days but she can be impregnated only during the night of the first day. You will have to introduce the male and the female to each other carefully every evening for four days until the correct day is found. This should be done under close supervision and on neutral ground, such as a spot on the floor, in a cardboard box or, ideally, a spare cage. Never under any circumstances put the male into the female's cage: this is her home and she will attack at once in defence of it.

When you select your breeding pair remember that they should come from different bloodlines and not be closely related. Then you can start to try and find an evening when the female comes on heat. When she is ready, she will probably go rigid, with her tail up and head held low. Both hamsters will start to run around the cage, with occasional stops to examine each other's genitalia. When the female finally decides that the male is acceptable, she will crouch and await his attentions. If they start to fight, return the female to her cage and try again the next day. Some breeders claim that a young female finds an older male more compatible.

A Long-haired Golden Hamster in search of food.

Only put the intended breeding pair together at night as, being nocturnal animals, hamsters prefer to do their mating then. Observations in laboratories have shown that most matings occur during the middle of the evening. Once mating has taken place, replace the female in her cage and leave her alone. Four days later, carefully introduce the female to the male once again. If she rejects him this time, the chances are that she is pregnant. If she comes on heat again, the mating can be repeated.

Place the pregnant female in a cage by herself and provide a nest box. This should be about 15cm square with a small opening just large enough for her to get through. Put wood shavings or special hamster nesting material made of soft tissue paper in the outer cage, not the nest box, as she will want to build her own nest. Do not even look into this nest until nine days after her litter is born. During her entire pregnancy, she should be left alone as much as possible. Keep cage cleaning to a minimum. Add more green vegetables and, of course, as much water as she wants. Now is the time to give milk, as she will benefit from this. This augmented diet should continue until she has weaned her young.

The birth of the young usually occurs at night and you can estimate it quite accurately if you know the exact time of the impregnation. It will be 16 or 17 days afterwards, never more or less. The newborn hamsters (which you should not see because they are in the nest and you should not look into it) are about 2.5cm long and weigh as little as 3-4g. There can be any number from one to a dozen, occasionally even more, but the average is seven. The babies are born naked and blind. They need no particular care and should be left entirely to the mother.

Warning: Don't even touch a baby except in an emergency. It is more than likely that the mother will resent the smell from your hand and destroy the baby. For the first nine days after birth, the little family should be left completely alone except for feeding or the removal of a dead animal. Only then should you start cage cleaning again.

Although the babies are blind at birth, the teeth are already formed and the body develops rapidly. By the time they are three days old, their hair begins to grow and the ears open on the fifth day. When they are eight days old, although their eyes are still closed, they will come out of the nest and wander around the cage, going to the toilet and eating solid food which their mother will offer them. Once they do start eating, be sure to increase the dry rations.

The hamster mother, if she looks after them at all, will take excellent care of her youngsters until they are three to four weeks old. However, the novice breeder should realise that some hamster mothers are cannibalistic and will eat their young, including the ones who die of malnutrition. This seems to be particularly true of first litters. Why this happens is not really known. It may be caused by unusual noises, a strange caretaker or voices, by inadequate quarters or unsanitary conditions. If a female should destroy both her first and second litters, it is unwise to breed from her again.

Some females die when giving birth because of a malformation of the pelvis which is common in runty females. Only well-developed, vigorous animals should ever be used to breed from.

By the time the babies are two weeks old, they will have a thick coat of fur and will weigh three times their birth weight. Hamsters do not open their eyes until they are two weeks old. At the end of their fourth week they should be weaned. At this age they resemble their bright-eyed parents and should be treated as adults.

When they are five weeks old, they should be separated according to sex to prevent premature breeding but each sex can be kept in a communal cage until they begin to fight amongst themselves.

Sexing Hamsters

Hold the animal on its back in the palm of your hand. The penis of the male is about 6-12mm from the vent. The vulva of the female is closer to the vent and is mostly bare, except for a few hairs. The general body contour is also an aid. The male presents a tapered, elongated rear, while the rear of the female is blunter.

A Black-eyed White mother cleaning her pups.

A hamster pup about six days old. The first nine or ten days in a pup's life are critical in terms of its development and survival.

MUTATIONS

In recent years many new mutations have been reported, the most recent of which is the Melanistic or True Black. Some others are:

Albino: The entire coat is pure white down to the roots and devoid of any shading or marking. The eyes are a bright clear pink. The ears are flesh-coloured and devoid of any dark patches. The gene is recessive which means that offspring are not guaranteed to be albino.

Dominant Spot: A white animal with a greater or lesser number of coloured spots covering the body.

Cream: An apricot or cream animal with black, red or ruby eyes. All ruby-eyed male hamsters are sterile.

Cinnamon: Lovely orange colour with blue-grey underfur. Nearly white belly and underside, dark red eyes.

Grey: Sometimes referred to as Dark Grey. Pencil grey colour ticked in black, with black cheek crescents and nearly white belly and underside.

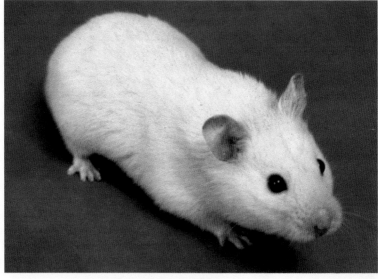

A Black-eyed hamster looks up with interest.

Silver Grey: A paler grey colour, somewhat similar to that of the chinchilla coloured rabbit.

Yellow: Lion-yellow colour ticked in black. Ivory belly and underside, dark ears, black eyes.

Tortoiseshell: If you mate a yellow male to a different coloured female, all the female offspring will be Tortoiseshell. This can be in either Golden/Yellow, Cinnamon/Yellow, Grey/Yellow or Black/Yellow, with or without white. The hamster is patched similarly to a Tortoiseshell cat. The gene is sex-linked, all Tortoiseshells being female.

White Band: The white band mutation was discovered around 1957. For perfection there should be an unbroken band about 5cm wide completely encircling the hamster's midriff. In practice the band is sometimes wider, sometimes narrower, but it is always sharply defined. The ears can be either dark or flesh coloured but in the adult only the bases of the pinnae (outer ear) remain without pigment. The rest of the ear is black. In some banded animals, there will be scattered brown spots along the mid-dorsal line. Eye colour is normal.

Dark-eared Albino: This is not a true albino because of the dark ear colour, although it does have pink eyes and snow-white fur. The eye and ear colour both darken with age. This mutation was first discovered in 1957.

You may wonder whether there are still more mutations to be discovered. It is possible, of course, but not too likely. Not all new colour variations are the result of mutation. Some have come from simple cross-breeding, such as the Dominant Spot and Cream creating the Cream Dominant Spot. Remember, too, that the entire genetic storehouse of our present-day hamsters goes back to that single litter discovered in 1930. No doubt we will continue to hear new reports because of the mounting interest in scientific hamster breeding. It should be realised, however, that the evidence required by a geneticist for a new mutation is far more scientific than that needed by the novice fancier. Genetics is a complicated subject, and too involved for this book. If you do become interested, there are books which explain it in more detail.

Nevertheless, if an unusual hamster does turn up in one of your litters and you are only a novice, report it at once to someone truly interested in colour genetics so that the strain may be perpetuated before it disappears. Unfortunately, this has not happened in the past, with the result that some mutations have been lost, perhaps forever.

HEALTH

A clean, dry cage is essential to a hamster's health. It does not like the damp and will suffer from it. A hamster kept in a small, dry cage that is cleaned often will remain in better condition than one kept in a large cage in which moisture, especially urine, is allowed to accumulate. Do not put drinking water in a bowl as it is almost certain to be spilled into the bedding material. Do not allow fresh fruits or vegetables to remain in the cage uneaten. They too can contribute to the unwanted dampness. If bedding does become wet for any reason whatsoever, replace it immediately with dry litter.

Make sure that wild rats or mice do not have access to your hamster's cage as they are carriers of all kinds of parasitic infection. When you buy a new hamster, make sure that it is in good health before bringing it into the same room as your other pets. Household pests such as cockroaches, bedbugs and mites often enter hamster cages. If you have to use an insecticide you must first remove the hamster from the cage. Put it in a temporary cage in another room. Disinfect the cage thoroughly, discarding all the old litter and replacing it with new, and do not return the hamster to the cage until you are sure that it is perfectly dry. It is unusual for a hamster to be plagued by mites or fleas but, if this should happen, commercial sprays are available which are formulated especially for hamsters.

Hamsters are susceptible to draughts and do catch colds (human colds and other respiratory infections), so any member of the family suffering from a cold should not handle the animals or even enter the room in which they are housed. If you have more than one hamster and one of them comes down with a cold, it should be isolated. The hamster's cold symptoms are much like yours: runny nose, sniffles, and general 'under the weather' behaviour. It is a sure sign that something is wrong if your pet ignores you when you call it for meals. Make sure that the cage is in a warm, dry and draught-free place. See that the hamster gets fresh water and give it a little cod liver oil. A couple of drops on a piece of stale bread are enough. Clean out all the old litter and replace with new, repeating this when the hamster has recovered to prevent re-infection.

A Gold Banded Hamster.

A Black Banded Hamster grooming itself.

The best way to tell if something is wrong with your hamster is to compare its present behaviour with normal behaviour. A healthy animal, on wakening, will run around the cage, wash itself, stand on its hindlegs, and climb the wire walls of its cage (though you should not expect this behaviour to last right through the day). The fur will be clean and smooth. Listlessness, dull eyes, no appetite, rough coat and general thinness are all signs to watch out for.

The hamster's greatest weakness is its teeth. They break off, get holes in them and are subject to decay. However, hamsters do have one advantage over humans: their teeth keep growing. That is why it is good to keep a branch of hardwood, such as oak or walnut, in the cage to keep the teeth worn down. Broken teeth caused by falls or bitten wire can result in the hamster not being able to eat, which means it could starve. If a tooth is broken, the adjacent teeth should be clipped with heavy-duty nail clippers so that they mesh easily with the broken tooth, enabling the animal to eat. The key to maintaining your hamster's good dental health revolves around providing vitamin and mineral supplements and hard foods to maintain the incisors. Your hamster should then be able to care for its own teeth.

If your hamster is caged by itself there will seldom be any cuts, wounds or bites to worry about. Hamsters in communal cages do fight, sometimes to the death, and that is why it is not recommended to keep them together after they have matured. As to wounds, there is no need to be concerned as long as the hamster can reach them with its tongue; the constant licking will prevent infection. Otherwise, treat any cuts with a mild antiseptic applied with a cotton swab. Do not bandage the wound. If it is bleeding freely, hold a bit of gauze firmly against it until the blood clots. A wounded hamster should never be kept in a cage with others as they are likely to attack it.

The hamster's droppings are also a good clue to its state of health. If they are rod-shaped and of normal consistency, all is well. Loose, watery droppings indicate too much fresh fruit and vegetable. Hard, dry droppings indicate not enough. Constipation is more common among young hamsters; make sure that they get plenty of fresh water.

Health Summary

Since the hamster is a remarkably healthy animal the chances are that you will not be faced with any major problems. If something does go seriously wrong and you are not able to handle it, isolate the hamster at once and consult your veterinary surgeon. If the animal is in great discomfort, and there is no effective cure or treatment, the kind decision may be to have it put to sleep.

BIBLIOGRAPHY

HAMSTERS
Percy Parslow
ISBN: 0866228314
TFH (1989)

CARE FOR YOUR HAMSTER, THE
OFFICIAL RSPCA GUIDE
ISBN: 0004125452
HarperCollins (1990)

HAMSTERS, FOR THOSE WHO CARE
Anmarie Barrie
ISBN: 079381376X
TFH (1994)

THE GUIDE TO OWNING A
HAMSTER
Anmarie Barrie
ISBN: 0793821541
TFH (1997)

PET OWNER'S GUIDE TO THE
HAMSTER
Lorraine Hill
ISBN: 1860540538
Ringpress (1998)

THE REALLY USEFUL HAMSTER
GUIDE
Lorraine Hill
ISBN: 1852791306
TFH (1999)

HOW TO CARE FOR YOUR DWARF
HAMSTER
Marianne Mays
ISBN: 1892791500
Kingdom (1999)

HAMSTERS, COMPLETE PET
OWNERS MANUAL
Author: Von Frisch
ISBN: 0764106546
Barrons

ALL ABOUT YOUR HAMSTER
Bradley Viner
ISBN: 186054021X
Ringpress

HAMSTERS, GETTING STARTED
Greg Ovechka
ISBN: 0866224122
TFH

We would like to thank the following for their help:
Hansard Pet Centre, Romsey
Denmead Aquatic Nursery, Denmead